MW01486912

A Garden of Flowers in Peyote Stitch

Sheila Root, PhD
Master Jeweler

©2017 Sheila Root
rootsbeads@gmail.com

Sheila Root is a beading artist and was in the bead business for over twenty years before leaving to travel and write. She has taught hundreds of students in seed bead techniques and basic and advanced stringing techniques as well as wire techniques. A former university professor with a PhD and degrees in design plus a certificate in Master Jewelry, she has been designing and selling "wearable art" for many years. Sheila also has a background in textile arts and was a founding member of FiberRoots and participated in many gallery exhibitions both in group shows and as featured artist. She has written several other books including:

Holiday Ornaments in Peyote Stitch (2017)
More 3-D Butterfly Patterns in Peyote Stitch (2016)
Flowers in Free-Form Peyote Stitch (2016)
3-D Butterflies in Peyote Stitch (2016)
Bird Patterns in Peyote Stitch (2015)
A Butterfly Garden in Peyote Stitch (2014)
Peyote Stitch for Beginner and Beyond (2014)
Spirit of the West: Amulet Bags in Peyote Stitch (2013)
Beaded Ornament Covers: A Beginner's Guide (2013)
Beaded Ornament Covers Book Three (2013)
Beaded Ornament Covers Book Two (2012)
Handmade, not Homemade: A Bead Stringing Guide (2012)
Wire Wrapping Stones and Beads (2nd Edition) (2012)
Graphics for Interior Space (out of print)

This book is one of a series of patterns for Peyote stitch. Watch for other titles coming soon.

Other Books in Peyote Stitch by Sheila Root

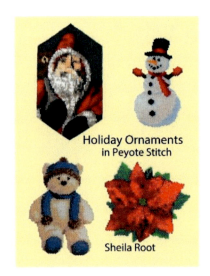

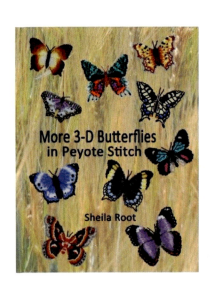

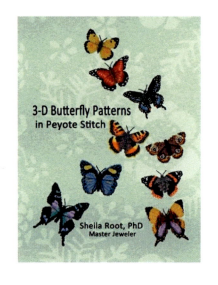

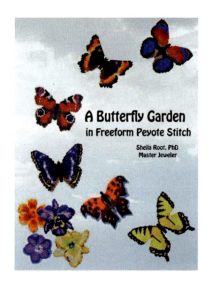

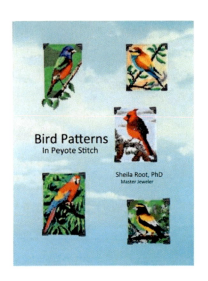

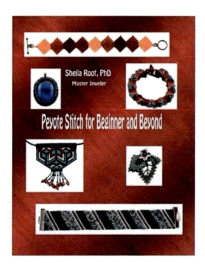

Contents

List of Bead Colors used in this Book
Page....2

Getting Started
Page...3

Pansy
2" x 2.2" (51mm x 55mm)
11 colors
Page...7

Pipeline Swallowtail on a Desert Rose
3.5" x 3" (83mm x 76mm)
15 colors
Page...10

Plain Tiger Butterfly on Cactus Flower
3" x 1.4" (77mm x 73mm)
11 colors
Page...13

Violet Spotted Charaxes on Clematis
3.6" x 3.125" (92mm x 79mm)
13 colors
Page...16

Blue Pansy Butterfly on Sunflower
3" x 3" (76mm x 76mm)
16 colors
Page...19

Redbase Jezebel on a Zinnia
3.125" x 3.5" (79mm x 89mm)
11 colors
Page...22

Cairns Birdwing Butterfly on a Wildflower
3.5" x 4" (89mm x 100mm)
16 colors
Page...25

Scarlet Mormon on a Clematis

3.125" x 3" (79mm x 76mm)
15 colors
Page...28

Tri-color Rose
3" x 2.6" (76mm x 66mm)
7 colors
Page...31

Water Hyacinth
2.875" x 3.25" (73mm x 82mm)
9 colors
Page...34

Appendix
Page...37
   Even Count Peyote Stitch
   Odd Count Peyote Stitch
   Increasing at Ends of Rows
   Decreasing at Ends of Rows

List of Bead Colors used in this Book: (number of designs that use the same color)

Yellow/Orange:

DB0751   YELLOW: OP MAT (2)

DB1132   LEMON: OP (5)

DB1133   MANDARIN: OP (1)

DB2101   LT LEMON ICE: OP DURA (6)

DB2102   BANANA: OP DURA (5)

DB2103   YELLOW MARIGOLD: OP DURA (3)

DB2104   CHEDDAR ORANGE: OP DURA (3)

Pink/Red:

DB0206   SALMON: OP GLZ (2)

DB0722   PERSIMMON: OP (1)

DB0723   RED: OP (2)

DB0727   LT SIAM: OP (5)

DB0874   CARDINAL: OP MAT AB (1)

DB2113   LYCHEE (PINK): OP DURA (1)

DB2114   LT WATERMELON: OP DURA (1)

DB2115   GUAVA: OP DURA (2)

DB2116   LT CARNATION: OP DURA (2)

DB2119   LT MAROON: OP DURA (3)

DB2120   DK MAROON: OP DURA (1)

Blue/Purple:

DB0217   AQUA: OP GLZ LSTR (1)

DB0356   LT MAUVE: OP MAT (1)

DB0728   LT THISTLE: OP (1)

DB0730   PERIWINKLE: OP (3)

DB0756   INDIGO: OP MAT (2)

DB1138   CYAN BLUE: OP (1)

DB1494   BRIDAL BLUSH: OP GLZ (1)

DB1497   SKY BLUE: OP GLZ (3)

DB1586   SEA OPAL: OP MAT (1)

DB1587   AGATE BLUE: OP MAT (2)

DB1588   CYAN BLUE: OP MAT (2)

DB2128   ROBIN EGG BLUE: OP DURA (4)

DB2130   UNDERWATER BLUE: OP DURA (1)

DB2132   DK CADET BLUE: OP DURA (1)

DB2135   DK IMPERIAL BLUE: OP DURA (2)

Greens:

DB0372   GREEN TEA: OP MAT GLZ (4)

DB0391   LT OLIVE: OP MAT GLZ (3)

DB2121   KIWI: OP DURA (1)

DB2123   FENNEL: OP DURA (4)

Tan/Brown:

DB0734   MAHOGANY DK: OP (1)

DB0865   FOREST BROWN: TR MAT AB (5)

DB2106   CAMEL: OP DURA (1)

DB2107   CEDAR: OP DURA (1)

DB2108   VERMILLION: OP DURA (2)

DB2109   CINNAMON: OP DURA (1)

DB2110   TOAST: OP DURA (1)

DB2142   COGNAC: OP DURA (1)

White/Gray/Black:

DB0002   BLUE BLACK: MET IRIS (1)

DB0010   BLACK: OP (7)

DB0200   WHITE: OP (6)

DB0871   BLACK: OP MAT AB (6)

DB1518   LT SMOKE: OP MAT GLZ (1)

Blue/Purple (cont.)

DB2136   CROCUS: OP DURA (1)

DB2138   LT ORCHID: OP DURA (3)

DB2139   MED ORCHID: OP DURA (1)

DB2140   DK ORCHID: OP DURA (1)

Getting Started

The flower patterns in this book are all original patterns not previously published elsewhere. All patterns are flat designs and have freeform edges. Freeform shaped designs in peyote stitch involve using increases and decreases at the ends of rows to create a shape with no background. Many rows will also have an odd number of beads, requiring the use of odd count peyote stitch.

The Appendix includes a refresher on even count and odd-count peyote stitch, increases and decreases.

Artistic license has been used in combining butterflies with flowers. Some butterflies may be more accurately portrayed in a mud puddle but a flower is a bit more attractive in beadwork. The size and geographic relationship between flowers and butterflies has also been chosen for effect rather than accuracy.

Following Diagrams

If you are making a rectangular piece in peyote stitch you can simply start at one end and work to the other end. With freeform shaped designs in peyote stitch it is easier to start in the middle and work one direction, then go back and work the other direction. Patterns are shown sideways to maximize their size on the page. If you start with a long thread with a bead stopper in the middle, you can work the top part then move the needle to the other end of the thread and work the bottom part. This will avoid a thread splice in the middle. (Remove the bead stopper after the first three or four rows so that you don't get your thread caught up in it.)

Section Diagrams: Each pattern is divided into sections to make it easier to follow the irregular shape. **Sections are worked in the order and direction of the arrows.**

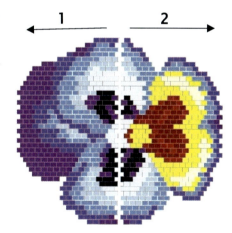

In the sample shown here, you would start at the division and work to the left and complete the first section. Turn the pattern and your beadwork over and work the second section. The first row of the second section is worked directly into the first row from the first section using the thread left at the bead stopper. The location of increases are marked by < or > on diagrams. (See Appendix)

The shape of the petals may require areas to be worked one at a time. In the sample shown here, work from the bottom up to the first line and finish off the wing section (1). Run the thread back through the beads to the point where you left off. Work up to the next line and finish off the small leaf to the right (2). Work to the next line and finish off the next leaf on the right (3) and then the leaf on the left (4). Run the thread back down through

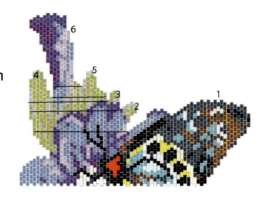

the leaf and work up to the next line (complete 5). When you have finished all the small projecting parts, finish off the flower bud (6). Before you end the thread, run it back and forth through the beads to reinforce the bud so that it doesn't flop over.

The pattern diagrams do not have these lines on them. Just work until you come to a gap in the beadwork and finish off the small area next to the gap before continuing up the flower.

Note: If you wish to work in **Brick Stitch** rather than peyote stitch, work the patterns sideways and ignore the space between the sections.

Needles and Thread

Thread: Peyote stitch in general can be pretty hard on the thread, but working a lot of decreases, increases, and odd count ends is even tougher on your thread. Choose a high quality beading thread (preferably braided thread) in a relatively fine weight. For a normal piece of rectangular even count peyote stitch a size D or 10 lb. thread and a size 10 needle work fine, but they are too thick for this kind of work.

Choose about a **4–8 lb. weight in a braided thread**. Flatten the end of your braided thread to make it easier to insert into the needle. You can use a white thread and color any edges that show with a permanent marker to match the beads along the edges. Never use sewing thread: it is not designed for this type of work and will not hold up. (The samples in this book are all worked on 8lb. Spectra fiber which is sold as both beading thread and fishing line.)

Needles: Also choose a smaller size beading needle, no larger than a **size 12**. Either beading needles or sharps will work. The sharps bend less but can be harder to find at your local bead store. Do not use sewing needles; the eyes are too big.

Working increases and decreases requires extra passes of the needle through many end beads and if your needle is too thick it can get stuck in a bead. If the needle won't go through a bead, pull it off and use a smaller size needle. Don't force the needle through since this can break the bead, especially if it is a matte finish bead. The matte finish beads seem to break easier than the shiny ones.

Beads

All the patterns in the book are sized for 11/0 Japanese cylinder beads. The color numbers given are for Miyuki Delica beads. The patterns can also be worked in other brands of Japanese cylinder beads but their numbers will be different. Use the photos of the color strips to help with substitution of colors.

The patterns could be worked in 15/0 cylinder beads for a more delicate version or in 10/0 cylinder beads for a larger version. Using 11/0 rocailles (round seed beads) instead of cylinder beads would distort the shape of the finished piece since the length to width ratio is not the same as it is for the cylinder beads.

Tip: Before you begin beading, **get organized**. It is much easier to keep track of your bead colors if you use a beading tray and label the bins A, B, C, etc. to match the color numbers on the charts.

Lay your ruler across the row you are working on in the diagram. Pick the colors from the beading dish and lay them out in order on your bead mat. Check off the row on the chart. Work the row from the line of beads on the mat. Repeat for the next row.

Color

The colors used in the patterns were selected to give the designs a more three-dimensional appearance in the flat pattern. Reducing the number of colors would make the flower appear as just a flat shape, more like a cartoon.

Many colors are repeated in several designs to help reduce the total number of bead colors needed for the book. Some designs require only a few beads in a particular color, but that color is almost always used in at least one or more other patterns.

Substituting Colors

All the colors used in this book are readily available online, if not in your local bead store. If you are unable to find the colors used in the patterns or wish to use beads you already have on hand, it may sometimes be necessary to substitute colors. A lot of trial and error has gone into selecting colors for the patterns because some colors or finishes just don't work well in this type of use.

Keep in mind that many colors and/or finishes look very different worked up than they do in the tube. Transparent colors, especially the lighter ones, may look like the right color in the tube but when they are worked into a pattern they look much lighter and often washed out. Some color numbers may also look like two totally different shades in the tubes but when they are worked side by side in small quantities the difference is so subtle that they look the same. Subtle color changes add realism as long as you can still see them.

Also maintain a balance of shiny and matte colors. If you use all shiny beads, especially silver lined ones, the pattern can just get lost in the shine. Duracoat colors and opaque colors work very well. They have a subtle sheen to them that shows off the pattern without looking dull. Matt finish beads also look good but they tend to break easier so be gentle.

To test your substitute colors, string a couple of beads of each color onto a needle in the order they will be in the pattern. If they don't look good on the needle they will definitely not look good in the pattern. If they look good on the needle, try working a small swatch of the colors together. If they still look good, go for it.

Substitutions of finish only usually don't make a difference. For example, if the pattern calls for Periwinkle OP and you already have Periwinkle OP MAT there will not be a big enough difference in appearance to need to buy another tube.

Changing Colors

Sometimes you may want to change the color of a flower or butterfly to match a particular color scheme. Select the new color palette in the same value range as the suggested colors: i.e. replace the lightest color with the lightest shade in the new color palette and the darkest color with the darkest shade in the new color palette.

Colors are listed by Delica number, color name and finish, and quantity needed to complete the pattern. If you are using a brand of Japanese cylinder beads other than Miyuki's Delica beads use the color illustration to substitute appropriate colors from your brand of beads.

Quantities are given in number of beads used in the design. Japanese cylinder beads are usually sold in tubes of 5 or more grams. One gram contains approximately 200 beads.

Abbreviations Used in Color Names

AB= aurora borealis	OP=opaque	MAT=matte	TR=transparent
MET=metallic	DURA=Duracoat	IRIS= rainbow	
S/L=silver lined	GLZ= glazed	LSTR=luster	

Pansy

Finished size approximately 2" x 2.2" (51mm x 55mm)

The Pansy is the simplest design so it is a good place to start if you are new to this type of work.

Letter		Colors Shown		# of Beads
A	DB2101	LT LEMON ICE: OP DURA		35
B	DB0751	YELLOW: OP MAT		56
C	DB1132	LEMON: OP		63
D	DB2120	DK MAROON: OP DURA		30
E	DB0734	MAHOGANY DK: OP		50
F	DB1497	SKY BLUE: OP GLZ		72
G	DB1587	AGATE BLUE: OP MAT		80
H	DB0730	PERIWINKLE: OP		210
I	DB1588	CYAN BLUE: OP MAT		156
J	DB0756	INDIGO: OP MAT		154
K	DB0002	BLUE BLACK: MET IRIS		51

Work the pattern sections in the direction and order of the arrows.

Line the second section up with the first as shown in the diagram here.

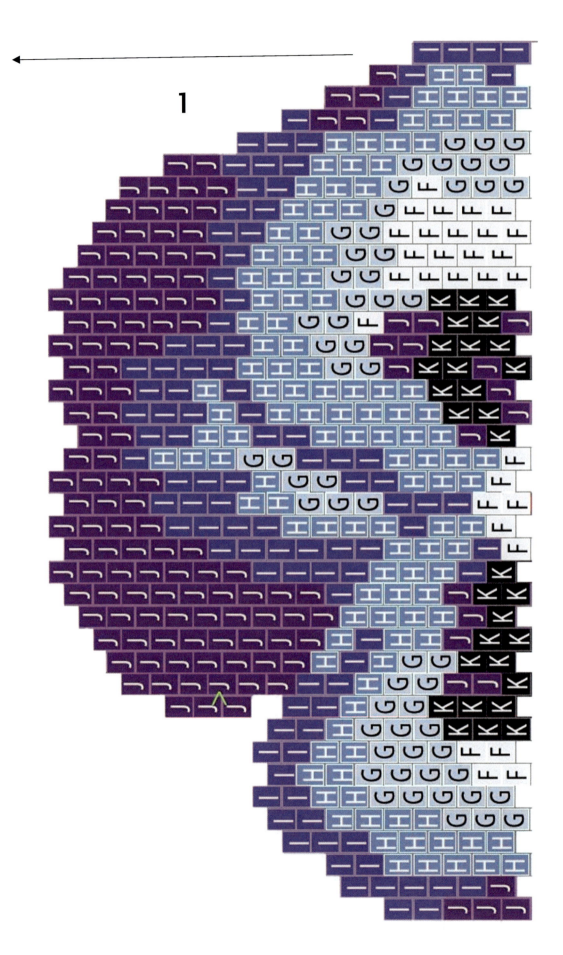

1

2

Pipeline Swallowtail on Desert Rose

Finished size approximately 3.5" x 3" (83mm x 76mm)

Letter		Colors Shown	# of Beads
A	DB2123	FENNEL: OP DURA	10
B	DB2101	LT LEMON ICE: OP DURA	41
C	DB2102	BANANA: OP DURA	37
D	DB0200	WHITE: OP	158
E	DB1494	BRIDAL BLUSH: OP GLZ	289
F	DB0356	LT MAUVE: OP MAT	199
G	DB0728	LT THISTLE: OP	110
H	DB0206	SALMON: OP GLZ	159
I	DB2116	LT CARNATION: OP DURA	153
J	DB2115	GUAVA: OP DURA	251
K	DB2104	CHEDDAR ORANGE: OP DURA	27
L	DB0871	BLACK: OP MAT AB	293
M	DB0010	BLACK: OP	137
N	DB2128	ROBIN EGG BLUE: OP DURA	43
O	DB2135	DK IMPERIAL BLUE: OP DURA	64

Work the pattern in the order and direction of the arrows. Match the two sections as shown here on the right.

1

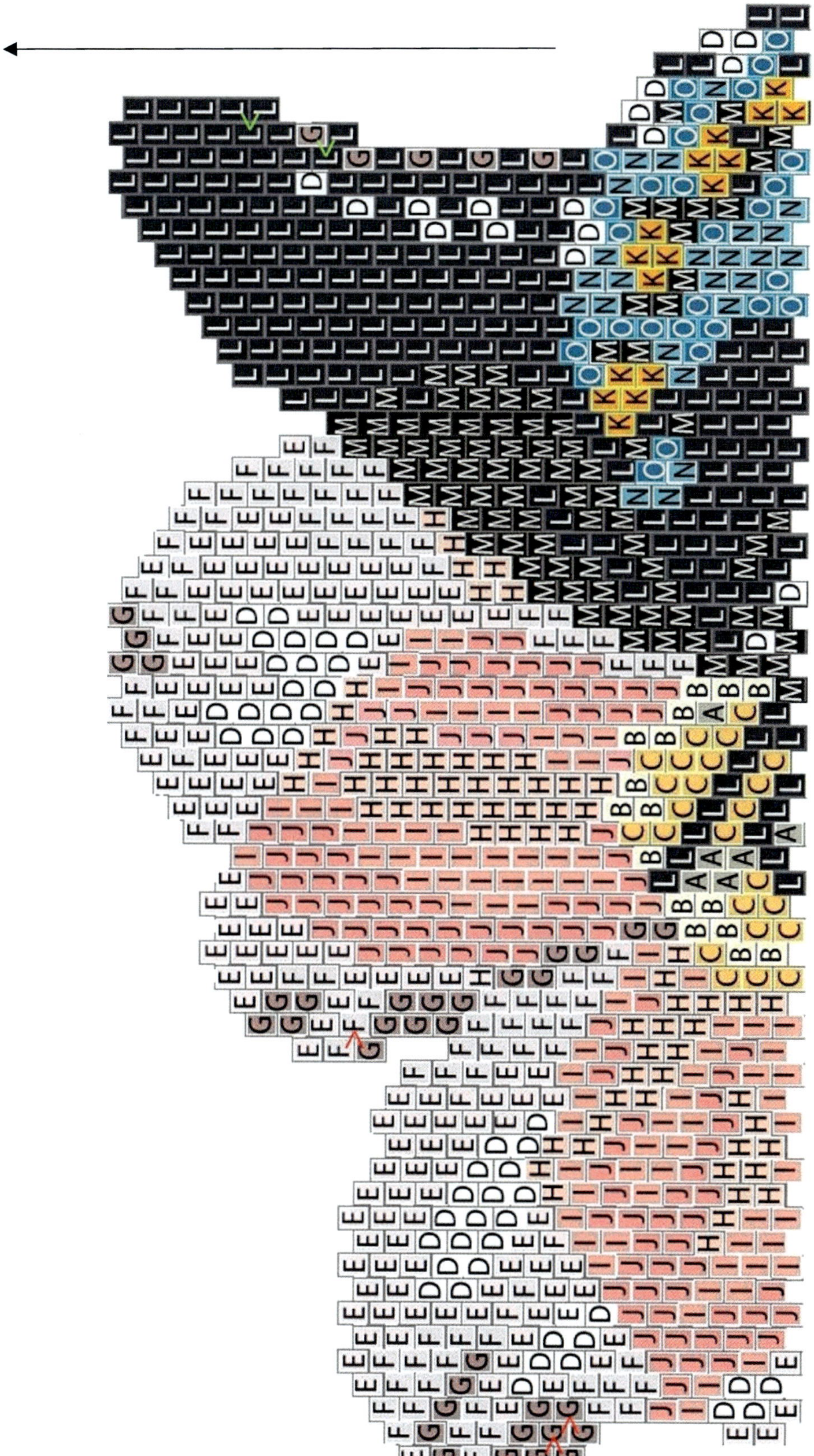

2 ←

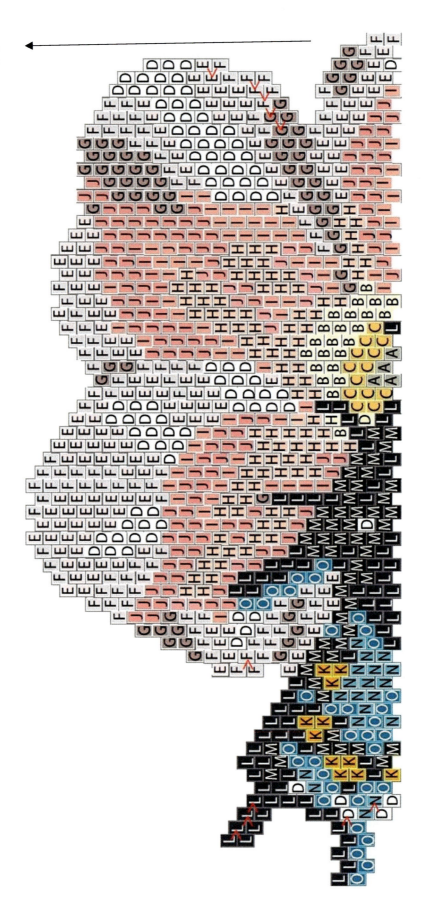

Plain Tiger Butterfly on Cactus Flower

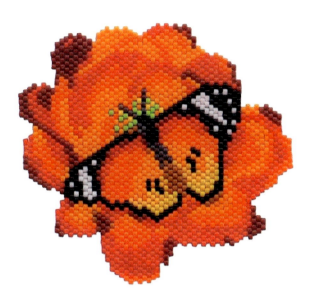

Finished size approximately 3.1" x 2.875"
(77mm x 73mm)

Letter		Colors Shown	# of Beads
A	DB2119	LT MAROON: OP DURA	176
B	DB0727	LT SIAM: OP	491
C	DB0722	PERSIMMON: OP	351
D	DB1133	MANDARIN: OP	327
E	DB2103	YELLOW MARIGOLD: OP DURA	35
F	DB1132	LEMON: OP	39
G	DB2108	VERMILLION: OP DURA	31
H	DB0200	WHITE: OP	38
I	DB0865	FOREST BROWN: TR MAT AB	24
J	DB0010	BLACK: OP	170
K	DB2121	KIWI: OP DURA	16

Work the pattern in the sequence and direction of the arrows. Match the sections as shown in the diagram at left.

1

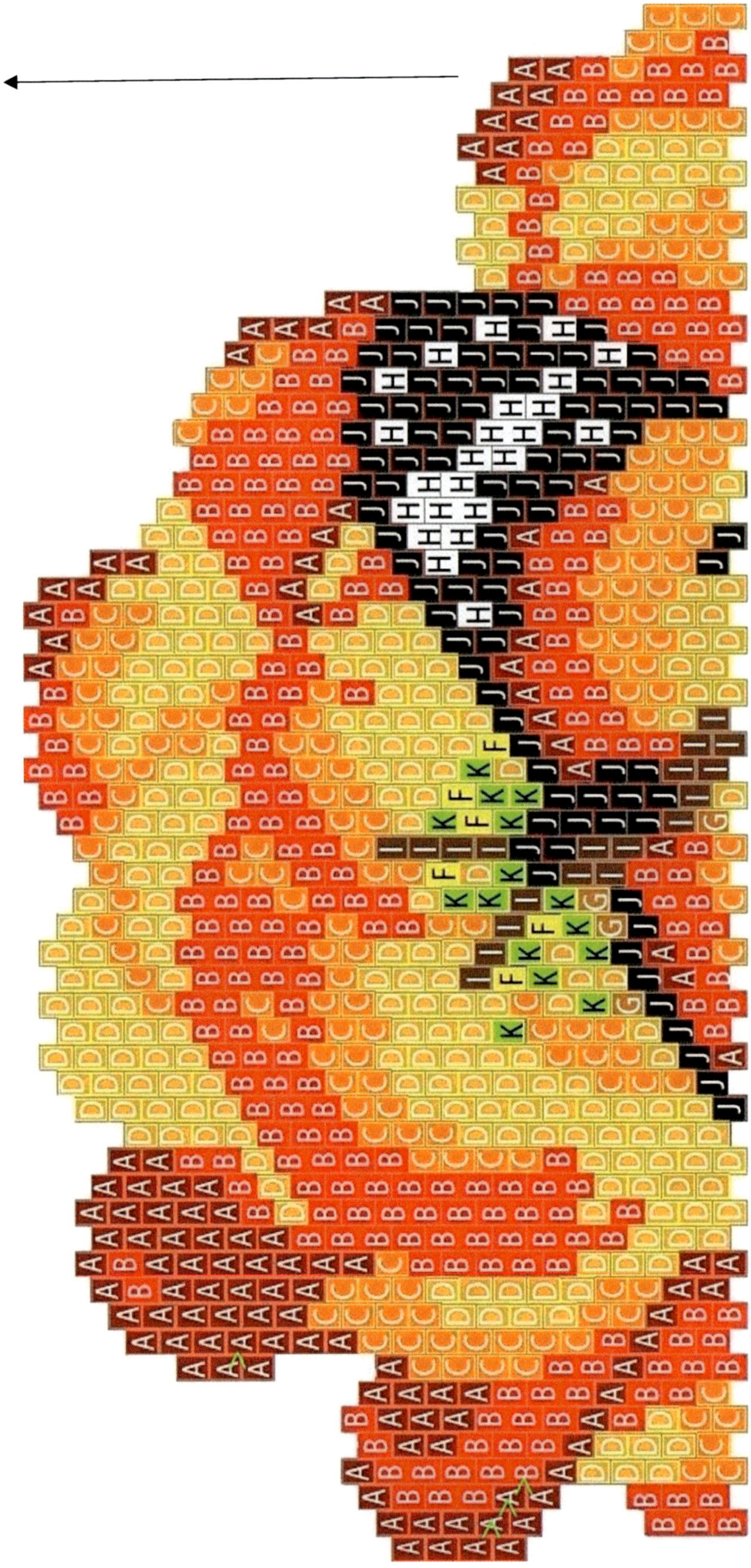

2 ←

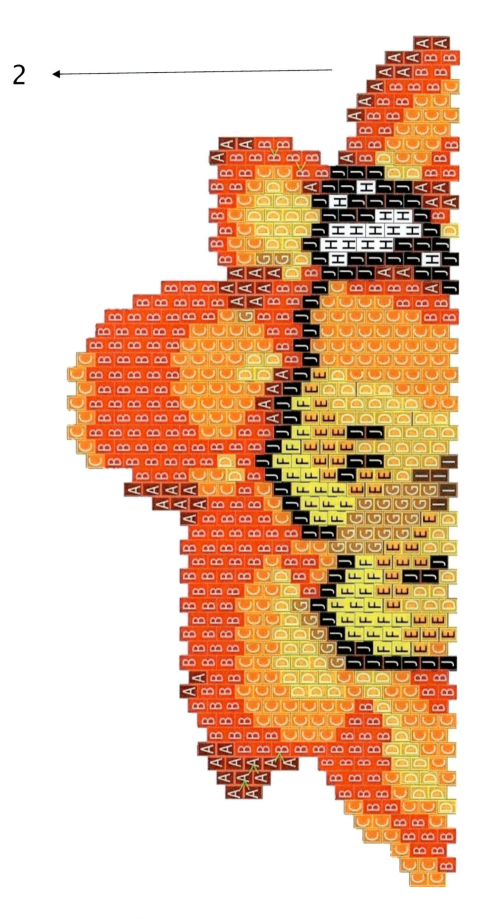

Violet Spotted Charaxes on Clematis

Finished Size approximately 3.62" x 3.125" (92mm x 79mm)

Letter		Colors Shown		# of Beads
A	DB2140	DK ORCHID: OP DURA		397
B	DB2139	MED. ORCHID: OP DURA		310
C	DB2136	CROCUS: OP DURA		260
D	DB2138	LT ORCHID: OP DURA		191
E	DB0372	GREEN TEA: OP MAT GLZ		67
F	DB2123	FENNEL: OP DURA		71
G	DB2128	ROBIN EGG BLUE: OP DURA		61
H	DB2135	DK IMPERIAL BLUE: OP DURA		58
I	DB2101	LT LEMON ICE: OP DURA		30
J	DB0200	WHITE: OP		22
K	DB0865	FOREST BROWN: TR MAT AB		26
L	DB0871	BLACK: OP MAT AB		30
M	DB0010	BLACK: OP		175

Work the pattern in the sequence and direction of the arrows.

Match the sections as shown in the diagram at right.

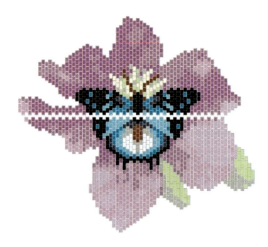

1

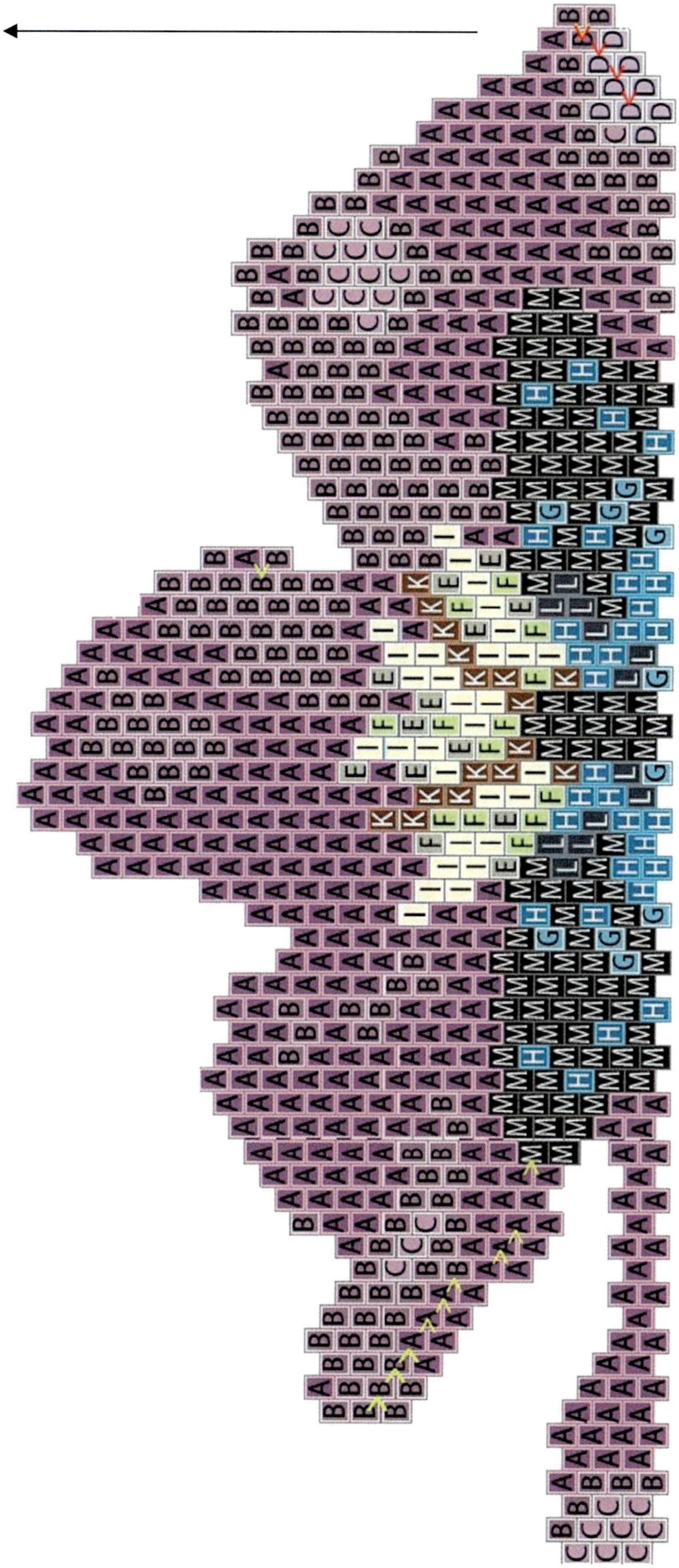

2 ←

Blue Pansy Butterfly on Sunflower

Finished size approximately 3" x 3"
(76mm x 76mm)

Letter	Colors Shown		# of Beads
A	DB0751	YELLOW: OP MAT	178
B	DB1132	LEMON: OP	424
C	DB2102	BANANA: OP DURA	360
D	DB2103	YELLOW MARIGOLD: OP DURA	99
E	DB2104	CHEDDAR ORANGE: OP DURA	96
F	DB2106	CAMEL: OP DURA	78
G	DB2108	VERMILLION: OP DURA	69
H	DB2109	CINNAMON: OP DURA	74
I	DB2110	TOAST: OP DURA	21
J	DB2142	COGNAC: OP DURA	22
K	DB0391	LT OLIVE: OP MAT GLZ	11
L	DB0200	WHITE: OP	22
M	DB2128	*ROBIN EGG BLUE: OP DURA	31
N	DB2130	*UNDERWATER BLUE: OP DURA	44
O	DB0871	BLACK: OP MAT AB	50
P	DB0010	BLACK: OP	262

*If the dye lots are too similar on M and N, choose a color for N that is slightly lighter than M.

Work the pattern in the sequence and direction of the arrows. Match the sections as shown in the diagram at right.

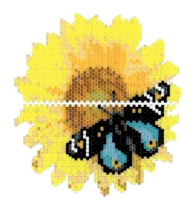

1

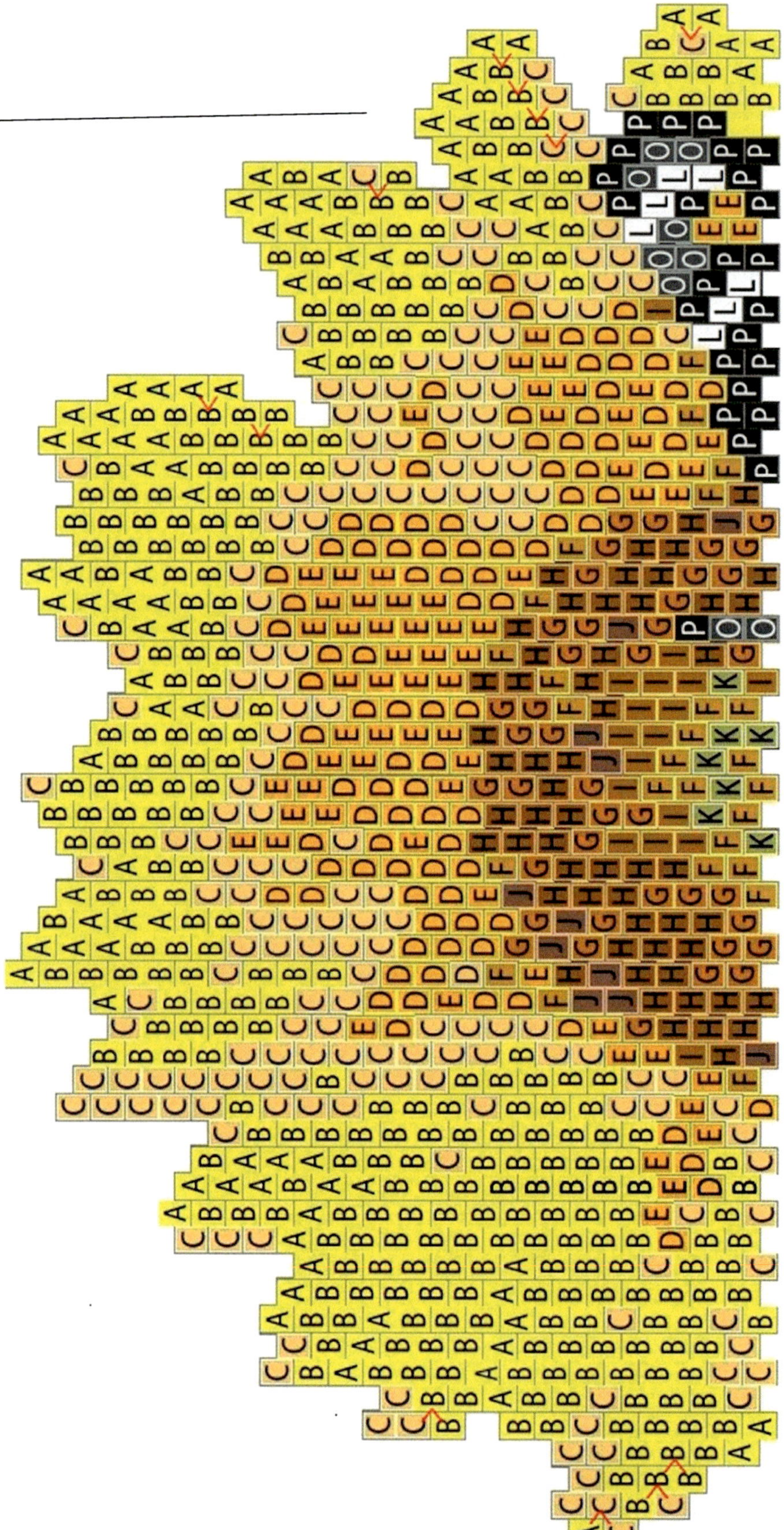

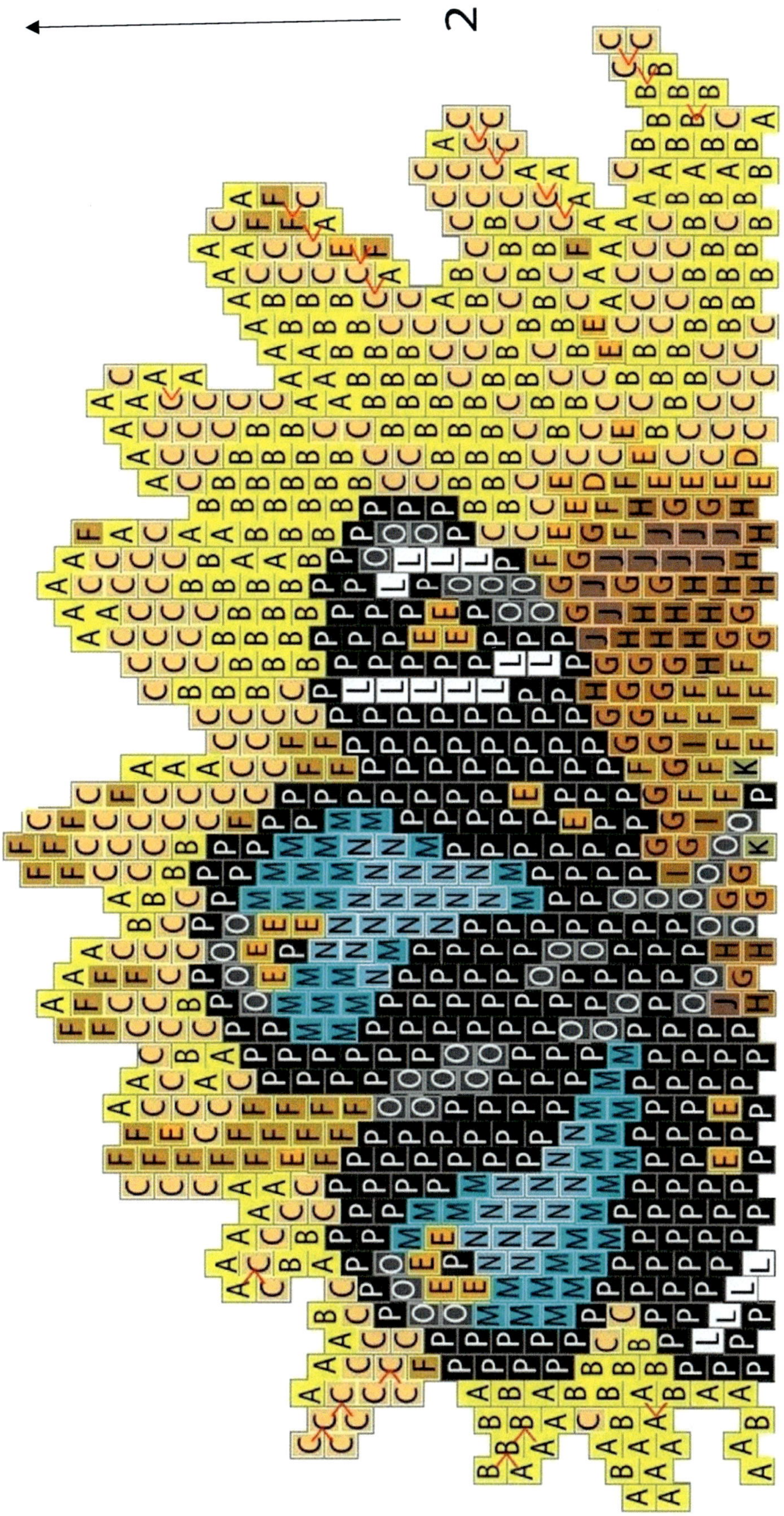

Redbase Jezebel on a Zinnia

Finished size approximately 3.12" x 3.5" (79mm x 89mm)

Letter		Colors Shown		# of Beads
A	DB2119	LT MAROON: OP DURA		220
B	DB0723	RED: OP		693
C	DB0727	LT SIAM: OP		391
D	DB2101	LT LEMON ICE: OP DURA		27
E	DB2102	BANANA: OP DURA		97
F	DB0372	GREEN TEA: OP MAT GLZ		67
G	DB0200	WHITE: OP		35
H	DB1518	LT SMOKE: OP MAT GLZ		22
I	DB0871	BLACK: OP MAT AB		91
J	DB0865	FOREST BROWN: TR MAT AB		33
K	DB0010	BLACK: OP		283

Work the pattern in the sequence and direction of the arrows.

Match the sections as shown in the diagram at right.

1

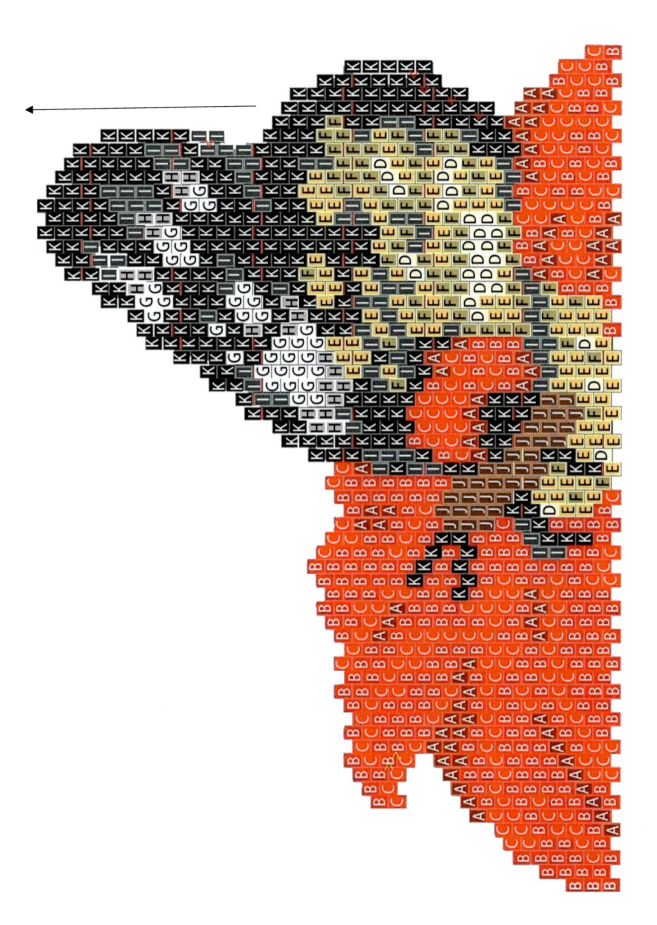

2

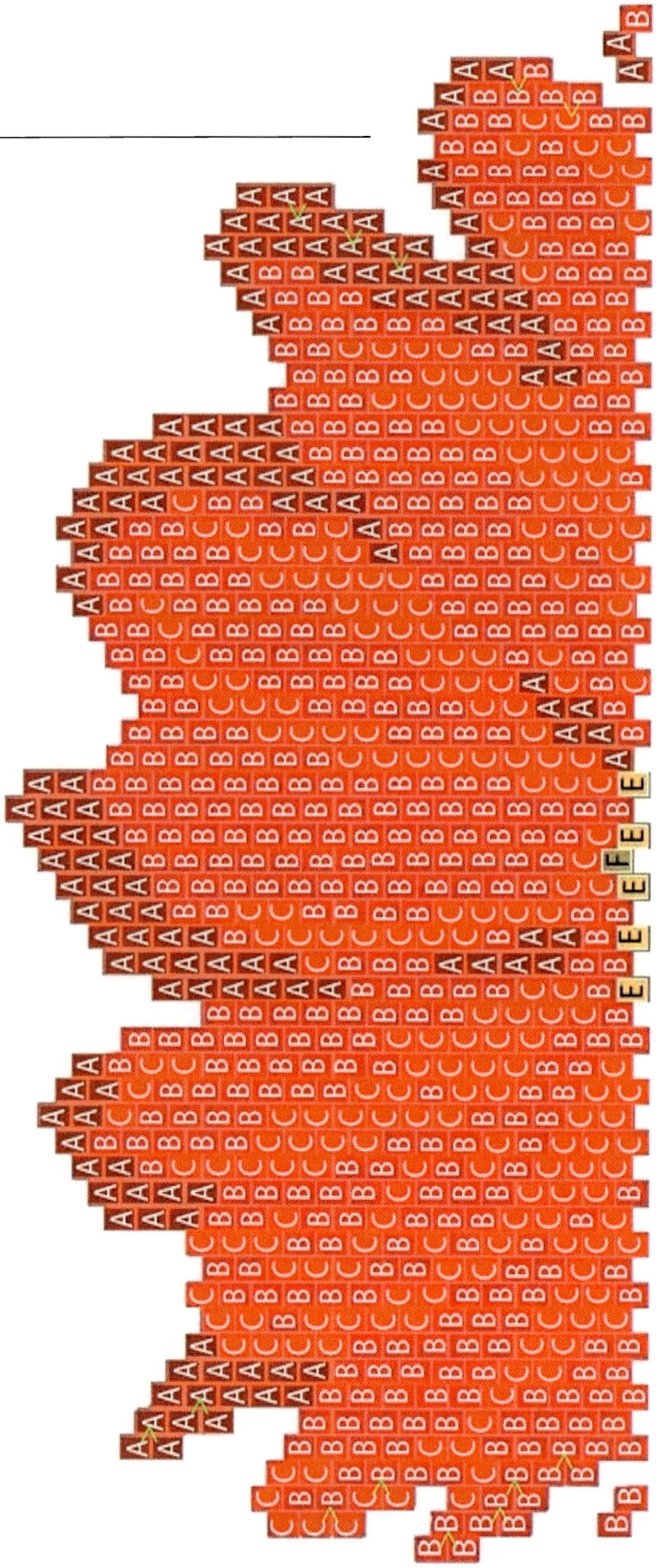

Cairns Birdwing on a Wildflower

Finished size approximately 3.5" x 4"
(89mm x 100mm)

Letter	Colors Shown		# of Beads
A	DB2123	FENNEL: OP DURA	46
B	DB0372	GREEN TEA: OP MAT GLZ	40
C	DB0391	LT OLIVE: OP MAT GLZ	103
D	DB2101	LT LEMON ICE: OP DURA	54
E	DB1132	LEMON: OP	60
F	DB2128	ROBIN EGG BLUE: OP DURA	64
G	DB0727	LT SIAM: OP	9
H	DB0200	WHITE: OP	19
I	DB1497	SKY BLUE: OP GLZ	51
J	DB0730	PERIWINKLE: OP	621
K	DB1138	CYAN BLUE: OP	359
L	DB0756	INDIGO: OP MAT	62
M	DB2138	LT ORCHID: OP DURA	103
N	DB0865	FOREST BROWN: TR MAT AB	99
O	DB0871	BLACK: OP MAT AB	170
P	DB0010	BLACK: OP	202

Match the sections as shown in the diagram below.

1

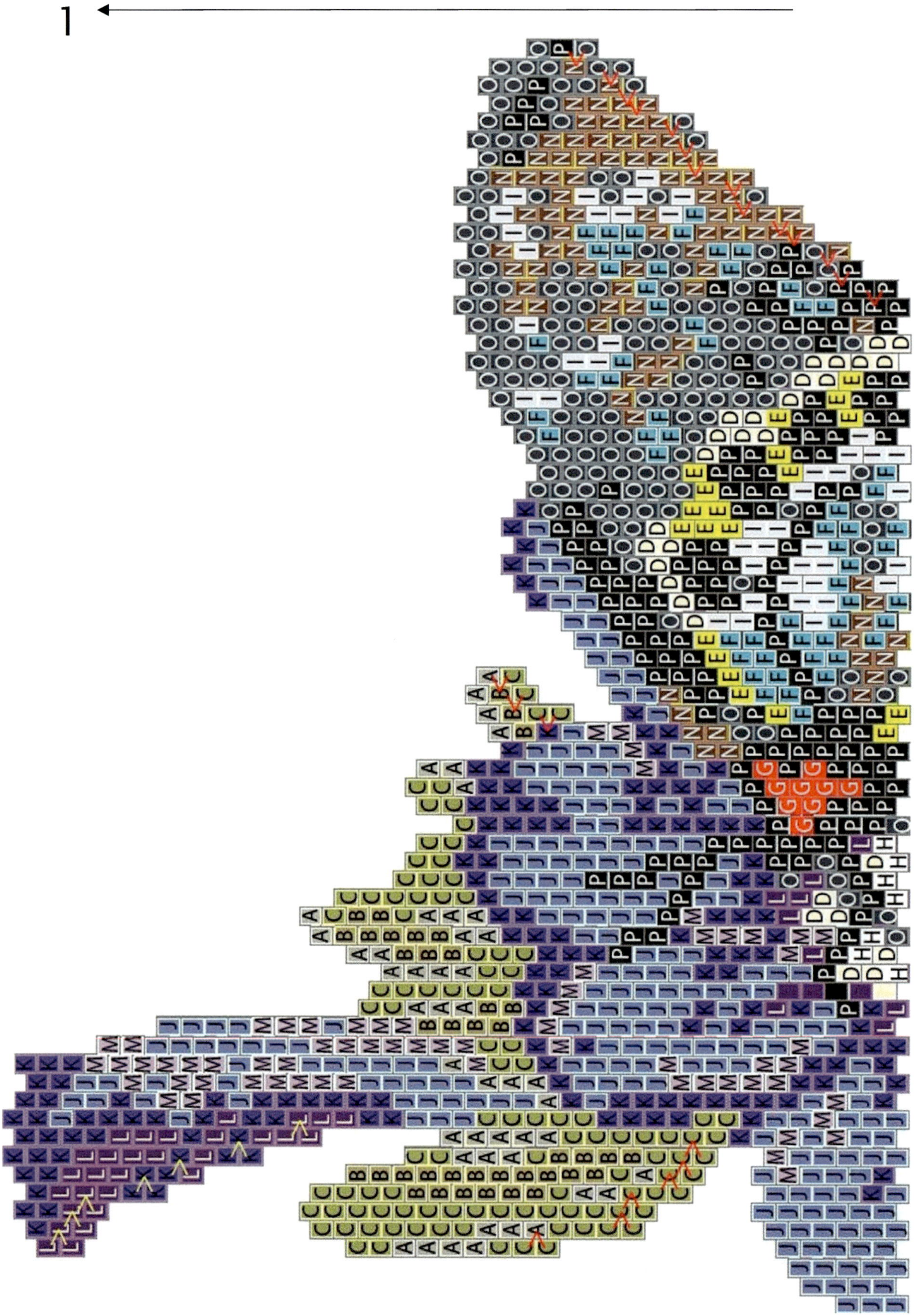

2 ←

Scarlet Mormon on
Pink Clematis

Finished size approximately 3.125" x 3"
(79mm x 76mm)

Letter		Colors Shown	# of Beads
A	DB2123	FENNEL: OP DURA	97
B	DB0372	GREEN TEA: OP MAT GLZ	105
C	DB0391	LT OLIVE: OP MAT GLZ	51
D	DB2107	CEDAR: OP DURA	40
E	DB2102	BANANA: OP DURA	23
F	DB0206	SALMON: OP GLZ LSTR	124
G	DB2113	LYCHEE: OP DURA	189
H	DB2116	LT CARNATION: OP DURA	157
I	DB2115	GUAVA: OP DURA	187
J	DB2114	LT WATERMELON: OP DURA	197
K	DB0874	CARDINAL: OP MAT AB	125
L	DB0727	LT SIAM: OP	78
M	DB0865	FOREST BROWN: TR MAT AB	39
N	DB0871	BLACK: OP MAT AB	90
O	DB0010	BLACK: OP	158

Work the pattern in the sequence and direction of the arrows.

Match the sections up as shown in the diagram here.

1

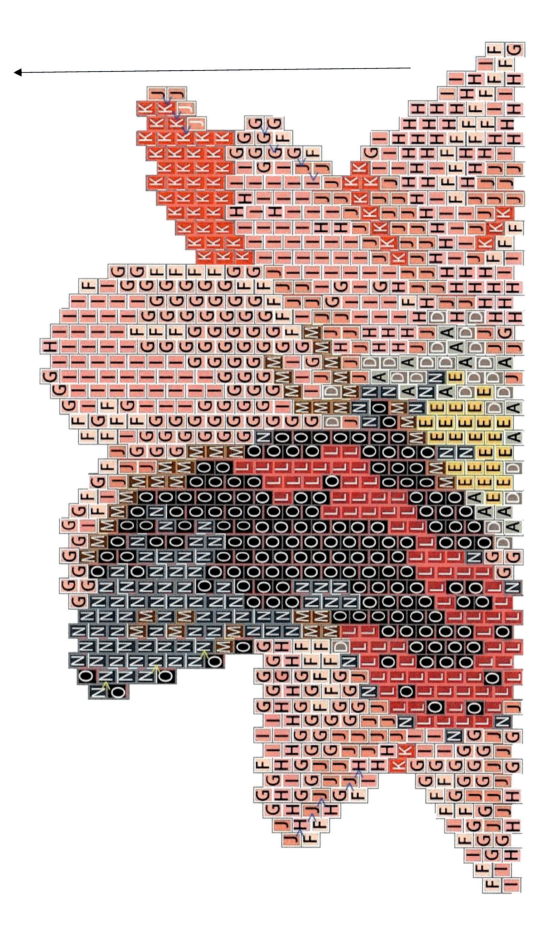

2 ←

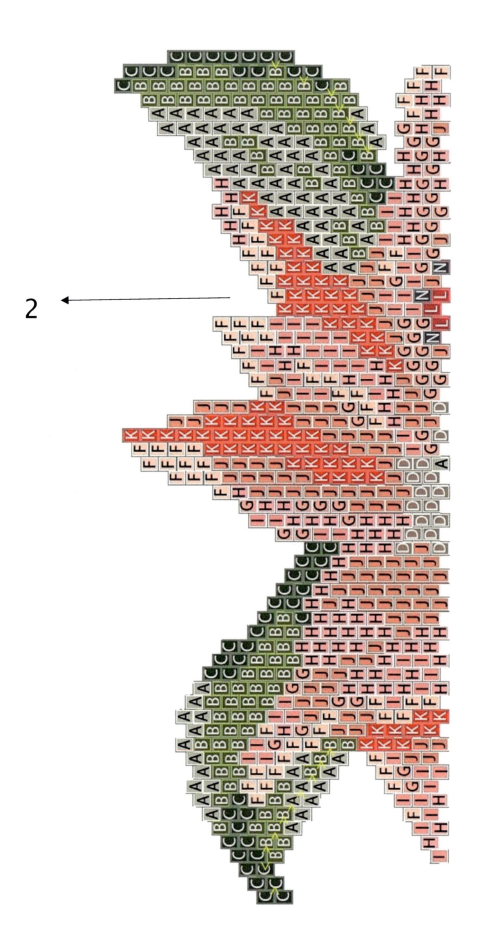

Tri-Color Rose

Finished size approximately 3" x 2.675"

(76mm x 66mm)

Letter	Colors Shown		# of Beads
A	DB2101	LT LEMON ICE: OP DURA	121
B	DB1132	LEMON: OP	200
C	DB2103	YELLOW MARIGOLD: OP DURA	132
D	DB2104	CHEDDAR ORANGE: OP DURA	254
E	DB0727	LT SIAM: OP	443
F	DB0723	RED: OP	259
G	DB2119	LT MAROON: OP DURA	142

Work the pattern in the sequence and direction of the arrows.

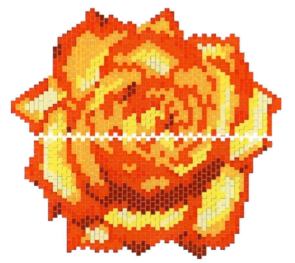

Match the sections up following the diagram

shown here.

1

2

Water Hyacinth

Finished size approximately 2.875" x 3.25" (73mm x 82mm)

Letter	Colors Shown		# of Beads
A	DB2102	BANANA: OP DURA	13
B	DB1497	SKY BLUE: OP GLZ	176
C	DB1587	AGATE BLUE: OP MAT	608
D	DB0217	AQUA: OP GLZ LSTR	405
E	DB1586	SEA OPAL: OP MAT	139
F	DB2138	LT ORCHID: OP DURA	133
G	DB2132	DK CADET BLUE: OP DURA	20
H	DB0730	PERIWINKLE: OP	85
I	DB1588	CYAN BLUE: OP MAT	43

Work the pattern in the sequence and direction of the arrows.

Match the sections up following the diagram shown here.

1

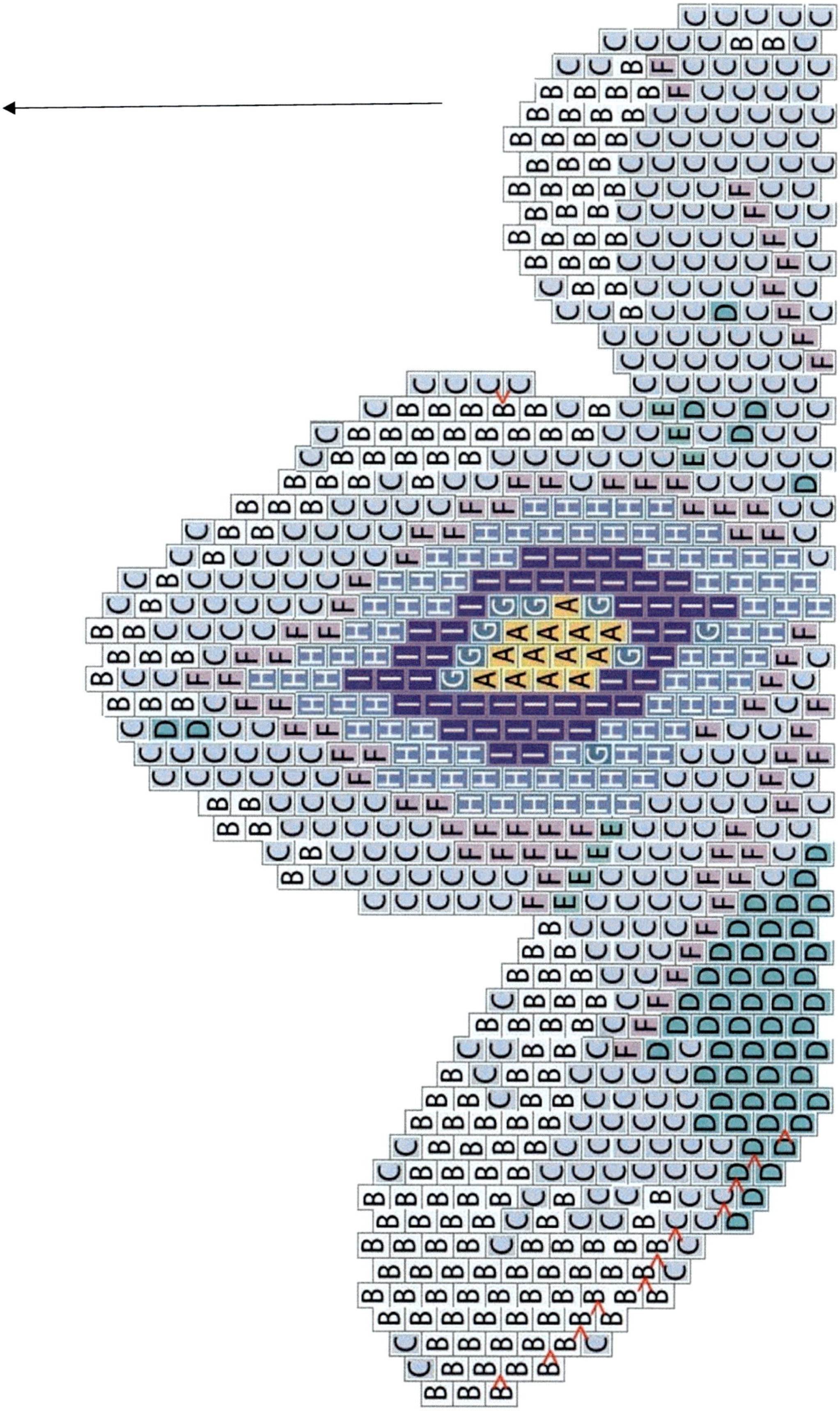

2

Appendix

Even Count Peyote Stitch

To begin, all the beads from Row 1 and Row 2 are strung on first, alternating the beads from the first and second row of the design. From that point on the beads are added one bead at a time. If the pattern is 60 beads wide you will begin by stringing on 60 beads; each subsequent row will then add just 30 beads.

Row 1 (green) & row 2 (blue):

String on all beads for row 1 and 2, starting with the first bead from row 2.

Row 3 (tan):

String on the first bead from row 3.

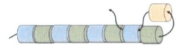 Run the needle back through the last bead from row 2 (2nd bead), skipping over the bead from row 1(1st bead).

When you pull the bead snug it will sit side by side with the first bead from row 1.

Continue adding the rest of the beads from row 3, each time skipping over the beads from row 1 and running the needle through the next bead from row 2.

Row 4 (yellow):

String on the first bead from row 4.

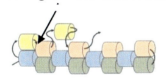 Run the needle back through the last bead from row 3.

Continue adding the beads from row 4, each time running the needle through the next bead from row 3.

Once you have completed row 3, the rest of the rows are easy because each bead from the previous row sticks up, making it easy to run the needle through the next bead.

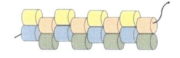

Continue adding rows until the piece reaches the desired length. If a pattern calls for a certain number of rows, remember that each row is ½ step up.

Odd Count Peyote Stitch

Odd count peyote stitch may be done with traditional techniques or with a two-needle technique. Which technique you use is a matter of personal choice. Either one will work with the patterns.

Traditional Odd Count Peyote Stitch: When working in odd count Peyote Stitch, there are two different ways of doing the odd-count ends of the rows. The edge will be nicer if you use Method 1 on the first odd-count row and then you can use Method 2 on the rest of the rows. If the edge starts getting a little out of line, do another row with Method 1.

Method 1: Method 1 uses a figure 8 stitch at the odd count end of the row. As shown here, the blue beads are row 1 and 2, the light beads are row 3, and the gold bead is the beginning of row 4. The thread will be running right to left in the light row 3 shown in the diagram. The thread path: A – B– C– D– B– E– A– B– C– D– F.

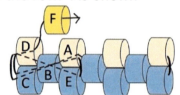

Remember that only one end of odd count peyote stich requires the extra stitch. The even numbered rows are started the same as in even count peyote. The odd numbered rows require the figure 8 stitch or Method 2, shown next.

Method 2: It is easier to use this simpler method of adding the end bead on odd count rows after you have anchored the first one with the figure 8 from Method 1. The thread will be running right to left in the diagram shown. The thread path: A–B–C–D–C–D–E.

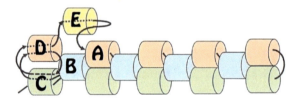

Two-Needle Odd Count Peyote Stitch: Two needle peyote stitch uses one long thread with a needle on each end. The beading is started at the middle of the thread, shown here on the right side of the diagram. One end of thread is shown in red and labeled "A" and the other end is shown in blue and labeled "B". Rows 1, 2, and 3 are worked with both ends of the thread.

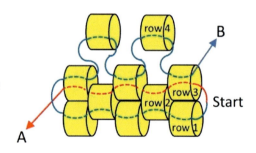

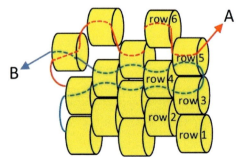

Thread end B is then used to complete rows 4 and five, then thread end A is used to complete rows 6 and 7.

Each time you exit the odd count end, switch to the other thread. If needed, you can use a clamp on the end not being used to keep the tension tighter.

Increases and Decreases

Because there are so many increases and decreases, we want to keep them as simple as possible. Most increases and decreases will be only one column (one bead width) at a time, however a few patterns do have multi-column increases. *The location of increases are marked on the diagrams by < or >.* The double end of the > shows the two beads being added and the pointed end of the < shows the bead where the two new ones are added.

To increase by one column on an even count row:

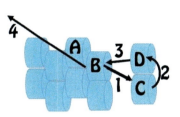

At the end of the even count row where you need to increase, exit from the last bead of the previous row (B). String on the two new beads (C & D). Run the needle back through bead B. If the added beads are different colors, check your diagram to make sure you have them in the correct order before step 5 and 6.

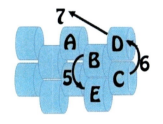

Exit from bead B. Run the needle through bead E and C (left to right as shown). Run the needle back through bead D (right to left as shown). Exit from bead D. You are now ready to begin the next row.

To increase by one column on an odd count row:

To increase on the end of an odd count row, it is easier to make the increase at the end of the odd count row above the row where you need the increase.

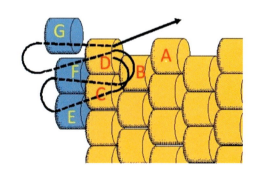

To increase at the end of the row ending in bead C as shown here, first work the row beginning with B (left to right) and the row ending with A (right to left). When you add the next to last bead of the top row (A), run the needle down through both B and C. String on bead D. Run the needle right to left through bead C. String on bead E and bead F. Run the needle through bead C (left to right as shown). Run the needle through bead D and F (right to left as shown). You are now ready to add bead G to begin the next row.

This sounds much more complicated than it really is. After a couple of odd count increases you will get the hang of it! Note that the new row now begins like an even count row. As you work increases and decreases the piece will frequently change back and forth between odd count and even count ends.

To increase by an odd number of columns (more than one): (This example increases by three columns.)

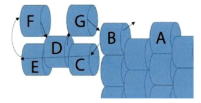

Working right to left, A and B are the last two beads of the row where you want to add. Exiting B, string on three more beads (C, D, E). Work back across these three beads in peyote stitch, adding beads F and G. Run the needle back through bead B and continue across the row.

For additional columns increase the beads C, D, and E by two or four more beads (keep it an odd number).

To increase by an even number of columns: (Example increases by two columns.)

On an even count end of row:

Row ending in A is right to left even count.

Exiting from B as you normally would, add on two beads (C and D) or any even number of beads.

Add on bead E and run the needle back through bead C and the bead below bead B, left to right. Run the needle back right to left through bead B.

Add bead F and exit through bead E.

You are now ready to add bead G to begin the next row.

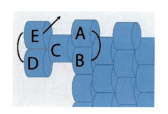

On an odd count end of row:

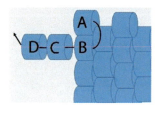

Add the last bead of the odd count row (bead A) as you normally would as in Method 2 shown in the odd count directions above. Exiting through B, add on the new beads C and D.

Add on bead E and run the needle left to right through beads C and B, then right to left through beads A, C, and D. Run the needle left to right through bead E and you are ready to start the next row.

To decrease by one column on an even count row: This method reduces the number of thread passes through beads.

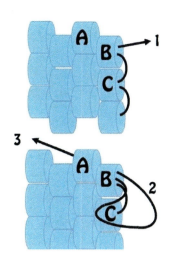

Exit the even count row through the last bead of the previous row (bead B) as you would normally.

Run the needle **under** the loop of thread between beads B and C. Run the needle up through beads B and A (right to left).

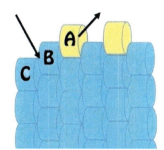

Note: When you pull the thread up tight, if bead A falls off you will know that you didn't go <u>under</u> the loop! Put bead A back on and try again.

To decrease by one column on an odd count row:

This is the simplest method to decrease on an odd count row. Leave off the bead that would normally be added to fit above bead C.

Run the needle <u>under</u> the thread between beads B and C (arrow). Run the needle back up through beads B and A. You are now ready to begin the next row.

Freeform shaped designs are constantly changing shape as you work, and because butterflies are symmetrical creatures, there will be an odd count finish, an increase or a decrease on most of the rows. As a result, odd count finishes will not necessarily all be on the same side of the design.

On some rows, if you were working the row from left to right, it would be a simple even count to finish the row and begin the next row above. However, if you need to work this row from right to left then you would have to treat it as a decrease and then the next row above would be an even count when worked back left to right.

Many of the flowers have an odd count beginning to the design but then quickly start in with increases and decreases. This can be cumbersome if you try to use a two-needle technique.

Tip: Start with two needles to complete rows 1–3 as shown below. Then run the top needle through the first bead on row 1 and run the bottom needle through the first bead of row 3.

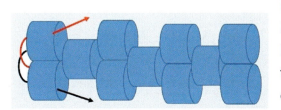

Proceed with the two sections of the flower with Method 2 for odd count. This gives you a nice neat beginning and is much easier than trying to keep track of two threads throughout the pattern with lots of increases and decreases.

Now that you have finished your garden of flowers and butterflies, what can you do with them?!

Here are some suggestions:

Frame them to hang on the wall

Decorate a cell phone bag or other purse

Sew one on your baseball cap or sunhat

Apply them like a patch on your jacket

Add a pin back to make a lapel pin

Use one as the center piece for a necklace

Decorate a special gift package

Use your imagination to come up with some wonderful ideas!